# Reach the Stars

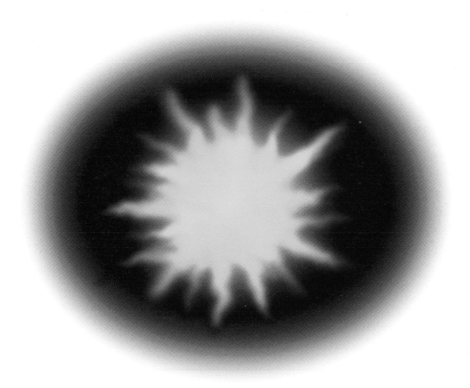

**Fiona Macdonald**

## OXFORD
UNIVERSITY PRESS

Great Clarendon Street, Oxford OX2 6DP

Oxford University Press is a department of the University of Oxford.
It furthers the University's objective of excellence in research,
scholarship, and education by publishing worldwide in

Oxford New York

Auckland Bangkok Buenos Aires Cape Town Chennai
Dar es Salaam Delhi Hong Kong Istanbul Karachi Kolkata
Kuala Lumpur Madrid Melbourne Mexico City Mumbai Nairobi
São Paulo Shanghai Singapore Taipei Tokyo Toronto

with an associated company in Berlin

Oxford is a registered trade mark of Oxford University Press
in the UK and in certain other countries

Text © Fiona Macdonald 2002

The moral rights of the author have been asserted

Database right Oxford University Press (maker)

First published 2002

British Library Cataloguing in Publication Data

Data available

ISBN 0 19 917457 1

Also available as packs

The Earth in Space Inspection Pack (one of each book)
ISBN 0 19 917458 X

Reach for the Stars Guided Reading Pack (six copies)
ISBN 0 19 917867 4

The Earth in Space Class Pack (six of each book)
ISBN 0 19 917459 8

10 9 8 7 6 5 4 3 2 1

Designed by Alicia Howard at Tangerine Tiger

Printed in Hong Kong

## Acknowledgements

The Publisher would like to thank the following for permission to reproduce photographs:

Associated Press: p 10 (bottom right); Bibliothèque de l'Assemblée Nationale, Paris: p 22 (left);
The Bridgeman Art Library: pp 15 (top), 27 (both); The Bridgeman Art Library/Ashmolean
Museum: p 10 (top right); The Bridgeman Art Library/Rachel Burr Corwin: p 29 (left); The
Bridgeman Art Library/Sidney Goodwin: p 23 (top); The Bridgeman Art Library/
The National Gallery: p 28 (top); The British Library: p 12 (top); The British Museum: p 23
(bottom); The British Royal Air Force: p 24 (bottom); Corbis UK Ltd/Bettmann: p 14 (top);
Corbis UK Ltd/Historical Picture Archive: p 11 (left); Corbis UK Ltd/Steve Kaufman: p 11 (right);
Corbis UK Ltd/Araldo de Luca: p 14 (bottom); Corbis UK Ltd/Francis G Meyer: p 29 (middle
bottom); Corbis UK Ltd/Roger Ressmeyer: pp 21 (top background), 22 (right); Corbis UK
Ltd/David Samuel Robbins: p 21 (bottom); Corbis UK Ltd/Stapleton Collection: p 12 (left both);
GeoAtlas: p 30; Getty One Stone: pp 19, 28 (bottom); Heritage Image Partners: p 18 (bottom);
The Image Bank: p 10 (left); NASA: pp 6, 7, 9 (both), 24 (top); Photodisc: p 18 (top).

Front cover: PhotoDisc

Back cover: Stapleton Collection/Corbis UK Ltd

"Evening Star" by Sappho (page 19), translated by Josephine Balmer,
from Classical Women Poets, Bloodaxe Books, 1996.

Illustrations are by: Stefan Chabluk, Celia Harte, Martin McKenna, Richard Morris,
Nicki Palin, David Russell, Thomas Sperling and Colin Sullivan.

# Contents

# What is a star?

A star is a ball of burning gas. Our Sun is a good example of a typical star. Like other stars, it is huge, measuring about 1,400,000 km in diameter. Also like other stars, it is astonishingly hot – its surface is 600 times hotter than boiling water, and the temperature at its centre reaches millions of degrees Celsius. All stars are a very long way away from Earth. The Sun is our nearest star, but even it is 149,600,000 km away.

▲ The Sun is a burning mass of gas.

## Starlight

We see the stars because they give off rays of brilliant light, which travel to Earth. Because they are so far away, they appear just as tiny, sparkling points in the sky. The beautiful, twinkling effect of starlight is produced when stars' rays pass through the Earth's **atmosphere** and the dust and moisture it contains bends or interrupts them.

Starlight takes a long time to reach us. Light from the Sun, which is close to us compared with all other stars, takes around eight minutes to travel to Earth. In comparison, light from Polaris (the Pole Star), which shines high above the North Pole, takes 680 years to arrive.

Polaris (Pole Star)

The Great Bear
**constellation**

▲ On a starlit night, travellers can use the Pole Star to guide them, as it always shines above the North Pole.

# Sunlight

The Sun's light is so strong that it stops us seeing all the other stars in daytime – although, of course, they are still there! We can only see them at night, when the sky above us is dark. This happens once a day, when the half of the Earth we live on has turned to face away from the Sun.

▼ The starry night sky with a full moon

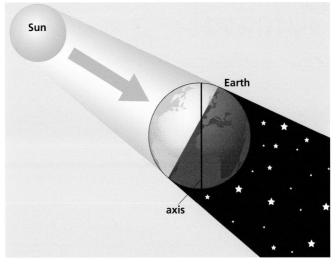

▲ The Earth rotates on its axis approximately every 24 hours, creating day and night, and determining when we are able to see the stars.

 **Star words**

When writing about space, we often use words based on Ancient Latin or Greek. This is because well-educated people used these languages in the past, and their scientific words have passed into our own vocabulary. For example, "astron" is the Ancient Greek word for star. Today, it forms part of the words "astronaut" ("star-sailor") and **"astronomy"** ("star-knowledge").

Here are some other star words:

**Astral** means starry, or about the stars. It comes from the Greek "astron" meaning "star".

**Scintillation** is the scientific name for twinkling starlight. It comes from the Latin "scintilla", meaning "tiny speck". Scintillating stars look like tiny specks of light in the night sky.

**Stellar** means very great or very famous. It comes from the Latin "stella", meaning "star", which is also a girl's name.

# Stardust

In fairy stories and pantomimes, witches and wizards sometimes sprinkle stardust on ordinary people, as a way of casting a spell. The stardust brings enchantment to everyone it touches, giving them magical powers, or sending them into a deep sleep while the world around them is transformed.

▲ A nebula is a huge cloud of gas and dust.

We enjoy these fantasy stories, but we do not really believe them. However, in the real world of science, stars and dust are linked together in surprising ways that are just as wonderful as magic and make-believe. Most stars begin and end their life as gas and dust. Strange but true, all living creatures, including us, contain some stardust which helps to make up our body's cells.

## A star is born

Stars are formed from atoms (tiny particles) of gas and dust that exist almost everywhere in space. When enough gas and dust collect together, they make a cloud, which gradually becomes denser. Eventually, the cloud collapses, and the atoms of gas and dust smash into one another, giving off light and heat. A new star is born.

# A star dies

After many millions of years, the star begins to decay. If it is small, it cools down. But if it is large, it gets hotter and hotter, and triggers off a tremendous explosion. For a short while, it blazes with extraordinary brightness. Astronomers call it a supernova – a new, super star. As the supernova burns, it scatters vast quantities of stardust throughout the Universe. Over time, these tiny particles of matter join together in chemical reactions to create new stars, planets, and living things – including human beings.

▼ The remains of a supernova

## Star past, star future

Like the stars themselves, Earth sends particles of dust out into space. This dust contains atoms that once belonged to living creatures, long since dead. It joins all the other dust in space, and is used to form new stars. Whatever their religious faith, many people find it very comforting to think that we were all once part of the beautiful starry sky, and that one day, we may become stars once more.

# Star life cycles

A typical star follows a life cycle that may last for millions of years.

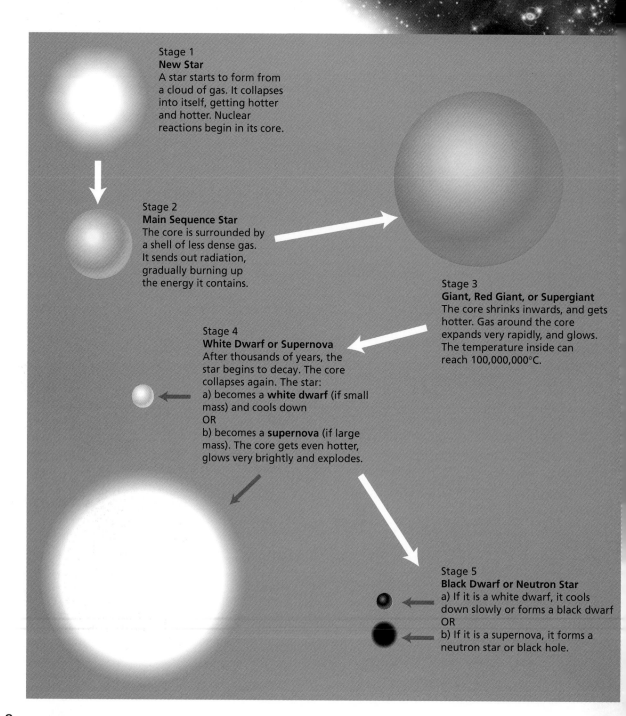

Stage 1
**New Star**
A star starts to form from a cloud of gas. It collapses into itself, getting hotter and hotter. Nuclear reactions begin in its core.

Stage 2
**Main Sequence Star**
The core is surrounded by a shell of less dense gas. It sends out radiation, gradually burning up the energy it contains.

Stage 3
**Giant, Red Giant, or Supergiant**
The core shrinks inwards, and gets hotter. Gas around the core expands very rapidly, and glows. The temperature inside can reach 100,000,000°C.

Stage 4
**White Dwarf or Supernova**
After thousands of years, the star begins to decay. The core collapses again. The star:
a) becomes a **white dwarf** (if small mass) and cools down
OR
b) becomes a **supernova** (if large mass). The core gets even hotter, glows very brightly and explodes.

Stage 5
**Black Dwarf or Neutron Star**
a) If it is a white dwarf, it cools down slowly or forms a black dwarf
OR
b) If it is a supernova, it forms a neutron star or black hole.

▲ A white dwarf

**Black holes** are created when white dwarf stars reach the end of their lives. (They may also be formed when very large, hot stars collide. Their cores are crushed together into a **singularity** – a place where the normal laws of science do not work.) Black holes are places where matter has collapsed under the pressure of its own **gravity**. The force of this gravity is so powerful that nothing can escape from it, not even light.

**Neutron stars** are very small, very hot, and very, very dense. They are formed when a supernova explosion comes to an end. They measure only about 20 km in diameter, but are ten million million times denser than water. Because they are so small, they do not shine very brightly and are almost invisible.

▲ The Centaurus A galaxy, seen here, is thought to house a massive black hole.

# The first star-gazers

Long before people could read and write, or use numbers to make calculations, they were able to observe and study the stars. They noticed how stars appeared to move across the night sky in a regular pattern, or when a new star appeared over the horizon.

▶ This pot from Iraq dates from around 3200BC. Its star motif suggests that star-gazing has been practised for thousands of years.

▲ Some Amazonian people used to believe that the number of rainforest caterpillars varied according to the position of the stars.

Some early peoples believed that star movements in the skies had an effect on seasonal changes in the environment on Earth below. For example, the Barasana hunters of the Amazon rainforest in South America named one **constellation** Caterpillar Jaguar. They thought that the number of caterpillars in the forest where they lived increased night by night, as the Caterpillar Jaguar stars rose higher in the sky. As a result of this belief in the stars' great power, they worshipped them as gods and goddesses.

## Measuring time

Before people had watches and clocks, they used observations of the stars to measure time. This tradition still survives today among members of several faiths.

Jewish people time the start of **Shabbat** (their day of rest) from the moment the first star is seen on Friday evening, and end it on Saturday at the time when three stars can be seen in the sky.

▲ A Jewish family celebrates the start of Shabbat

# Sky-goddess

▲ Nut is often shown stretching above the earth god Geb to form the heavens.

The Egyptians honoured Nut, goddess of the starry skies. They believed that she swallowed the Sun each evening and gave birth to it again every morning. They prayed to her for protection, and believed that she could help them live forever. The Egyptians also believed that they could be re-born as stars.

The Ancient Egyptians also worshipped the Nile Star (known today as Sirius or the Dog Star) and waited anxiously for its first appearance in the dawn sky each year.

For them, this was a sign that the River Nile would flood as usual, bringing water to their fields, which would help their crops to grow.

In Australia, the Aboriginal people recognize the "Ancestors" in certain patterns among the stars. They believe that the Ancestors created their world.

 An Aboriginal rock painting of a female Ancestor

## ✳ Scientific star-gazers ✳

**The Babylonians**, from the Middle East, and the Ancient Greeks, from the Mediterranean region, were two of the earliest peoples to make scientific observations of the stars. The Babylonians were expert mathematicians and used their skills to make accurate predictions about the movements of the Sun, Moon, and stars. From around 1800 BC, they kept remarkably detailed records of what they saw in the night sky. These records are still studied by **astronomers** today.

**The Greeks** had a different purpose for studying the stars. From around 600 BC, they tried to find out how the Universe was made and to explain how it worked. They made many important discoveries – for example, that the Earth was round, not flat.

# Stories in the sky

In the past, many different peoples have seen pictures in the stars. Often, they have linked groups of stars together in their mind's eye to form imaginary portraits of brave heroes, beautiful women, splendid animals, or horrible monsters. These star-pictures are known as **constellations**, which means "stars together". Although, from Earth, they appear to be linked together, the stars making up each constellation have no real connection in space. Often, they are many millions of kilometres apart.

▲ This picture of the constellation of Perseus and Andromeda was drawn in 1725.

▲ This image of the constellation of Capricorn was made in 1603.

▲ A Chinese map of the night sky showing several different constellations

## Star names and numbers

**Astronomers** today still use the constellations as a convenient way of identifying some of the biggest and brightest stars in the sky. They have divided the skies north and south of the Equator into 88 regions, each named after the chief constellation it contains: 48 of the constellations have Ancient Greek names; the rest have names added later by explorers and astronomers. Stars in each region are given names based on their constellation. The brightest stars are named with letters of the Greek alphabet as well. Faint stars are given numbers.

# THE COWHERD AND THE WEAVING GIRL
## A star story from China

Around 2900 BC, two bright stars, which Chinese astronomers called the Cowherd and the Weaving Girl, appeared so close together in the sky that they were almost touching. Looking up, and marvelling at the sight, people said that the stars had fallen in love and would soon get married.

Over the centuries, the Universe expanded, Earth's path around the Sun wobbled a little, and the two stars no longer seemed so close together. So Chinese people made up a fantastic tale to explain what had happened. They told how the Weaving Girl was so happy at being in love that she forgot to do her work. To punish her, the Sun-God parted the young couple and sent the Cowherd to live on the far side of the Heavenly River. (This was the Chinese name for the band of stars known today as the Milky Way.) There was no bridge across the river, and it seemed as if the Cowherd and the Weaving Girl would be parted forever. They were broken-hearted.

Seeing their tears, the Sun-God took pity on them. Once a year, on the seventh day of the seventh month, he ordered a flock of magpies to make a bridge across the Heavenly River, so that the Weaving Girl could cross it and find the Cowherd. But she could not do this if it was raining. To help the Weaving Girl meet the young man she loved, Chinese women prayed for fine weather on that night, and made offerings of rice cakes and watermelons to the powerful Sun-God.

# The zodiac

Star-gazers in many ancient civilizations, from Central America to China, believed that the movements of stars in the sky could forecast events on Earth. They thought that everything in the Universe was connected, from the smallest plant or insect, to the largest star. Change in one part of the Universe would, sooner or later, affect it all. Any movements in the stars would lead to changes throughout the Universe – including people's lives.

Star-gazers hoped that, by watching and recording movements in the stars, they could warn people of events that might happen in the future, so they could make suitable plans.

▲ This Egyptian zodiac calendar wa used by Greek scholars in Alexandr Egypt, to study the stars.

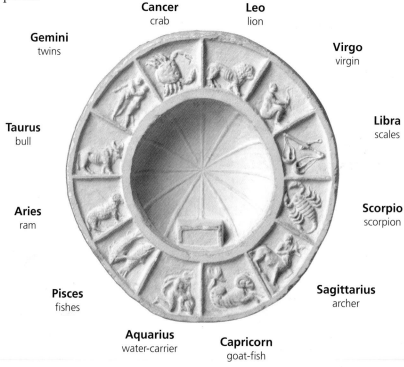

Cancer
crab

Leo
lion

Gemini
twins

Virgo
virgin

Taurus
bull

Libra
scales

Aries
ram

Scorpio
scorpion

Pisces
fishes

Sagittarius
archer

Aquarius
water-carrier

Capricorn
goat-fish

▲ The Ancient Greek and Egyptian star map was divided into twelve sections. Each section related to a period of roughly four weeks of the year, and each one was linked to a constellation visible at that time each year. Star-gazers called this chart a **zodiac** – a Greek word meaning "set of creatures".

They made lists and tables, and drew charts showing the expected movement of the Sun and stars across the sky. They also observed the stars at the moment a new baby was born, believing that star movements would shape the baby's future.

Some time between 300 BC and 30 BC, Greek and Egyptian star-gazers made a circular map showing the yearly changes in the Sun's position, as they observed it from Earth. They believed these changes were caused by the Sun moving around the Earth. Today, we know that the Sun appears to move across the sky because the Earth is travelling in an **orbit** around it.

Over the years, star-gazers and ordinary people came to believe that people "born under" the sign of a particular **constellation** developed similar characteristics, and shared similar prospects. Around AD 1600, the study of the stars became divided between two groups. Scientists, called **astronomers**, used mathematical and scientific techniques to make precise observations. Fortune-tellers, called **astrologers**, used traditional, unscientific beliefs and **superstitions** to make predictions about the future. Today, some people still believe in astrological predictions based on the zodiac – although they have never been proved scientifically.

People living in different parts of the world have different names for the signs of the zodiac.

▲ A zodiac chart from Sri Lanka, which includes many of the same signs as the zodiac used in the West.

▲ Part of the Chinese zodiac, which includes animal characters from Chinese mythology. Each Chinese year is linked to a different sign in turn. The year 2000 was the Year of the Dragon.

# Signs of the zodiac

The Egyptian–Greek **zodiac** is still used in many parts of the world today. It has its roots in the ancient cultures of the Mediterranean area – Ancient Egypt, Greece, and Rome. The signs have the Latin names given by the Romans. They are based on characters from Ancient Greek myths.

**Gemini**
**(The Heavenly Twins)**
*21 May – 21 June*

The twins Castor and Polyduces were two young Greek heroes who guided sailors at sea. They chose to die together, rather than be separated.

**Taurus** (Bull)
*20 April – 20 May*

Zeus, king of the gods, disguised himself by changing into this shape in order to carry away Princess Europa.

**Aries** (Ram)
*21 March – 19 April*

Greek hero Jason and his crew, the Argonauts, searched for the Golden Fleece of this ram.

Sagittariu

Leo

**Pisces** (Two Fishes)
*19 February – 20 March*

These fishes helped Aphrodite, who was the Greek goddess of love, escape from a sea-monster with her son Eros.

**Aquarius** (Water-carrier)
*20 January – 18 February*

Ganymede was a handsome young nobleman who became **cupbearer** to the Greek gods.

**Capricorn** (Goat)
*22 December – 19 January*

The Ancient Greek god Pan changed himself into a goat and was made a **constellation** by the god Zeus.

### Cancer (Crab)
*22 June – 22 July*

This was the crab that attacked the foot of the Greek hero Heracles, while he fought a monster lion.

### Leo (Lion)
*23 July – 22 August*

This man-eating lion, born of monster parents, was killed by the Greek hero Heracles.

### Virgo (Virgin)
*23 August – 22 September*

She was the daughter of the god Zeus, guardian of justice.

**Orion**

**Gemini**

### Libra (Scales)
*23 September – 23 October*

These were the symbol of justice and fairness.

### Sagittarius (Archer)
*22 November – 21 December*

Chiron was a wise and kindly **centaur** (half man, half horse), who helped to educate the Greek hero Achilles.

### Scorpio (Scorpion)
*24 October – 21 November*

This poisonous creature was sent by the gods to kill the Greek hero Orion, the mighty hunter, after he had boasted that he could kill any living thing.

# Some special stars

As well as observing the **constellations**, early star-gazers also watched and recorded the most remarkable single stars in the sky. They gave them names, told stories about them, and sometimes claimed they had special powers. Many of the most spectacular stars have Arabic names, because Muslim scholars in North Africa and the Middle East first recorded them, over 1000 years ago.

▲ These 17th-century Muslim astronomers are studying the stars with a telescope.

▲ One brilliant, pure white star was called Al Dhanab al Dajajah (The Hen's Tail), because it lay at the tail of a bird-shaped constellation. Today, its name has been shortened to Deneb, and modern astronomers call the constellation it lies in "The Swan".

In ancient Persia, over 2500 years ago, scholars claimed that four especially beautiful stars acted as the "Guardians of the Heavens". These stars also lent their majesty to the kings who ruled the mighty Persian Empire. Today, these stars are called by the impressive names Regulus, Aldebaran, Fomalhaut, and Antares. They are all exceptionally bright. Like kings and queens on Earth, they stand out in the crowd!

# The Evening Star

Hesperus, you bring everything that
the light-tinged dawn has scattered;
you bring the sheep, you bring the goat, you bring
the child back to its mother

This poem was written over 2500 years ago
in Ancient Greece, by a famous poet called Sappho.
She calls the Evening Star "Hesperus", its Greek name.

## The Evening Star

People in many countries have honoured the Evening Star – a bright "star" that appears low in the western sky, just as daylight is fading. Today, we know that the Evening Star is, in fact, the planet Venus, but people in the past did not realize this. They believed that the Evening Star guided wanderers home. For some lucky people, it also brought love.

## The Milky Way

Our Earth, the Sun, and all its planets lie within a spiral **galaxy** called the **Milky Way**. It measures 100,000 light-years from side to side, and contains about 100 billion stars. The Milky Way was given its name by the Ancient Greeks, because they thought it looked like a broad band of pale, milky light stretching across the dark night sky. (The name "galaxy" comes from the Greek word for milk, "galaktos".) Greek legends told how heavenly milk spilled across the sky from the breast of the goddess Hera, as she was feeding her baby son, Heracles.

▲ The Milky Way galaxy seen in the night sky has a hazy white appearance.

# Steering by the stars

Today, sailors, pilots, and explorers crossing wide, featureless deserts can rely on many different inventions – such as magnetic compasses, radar, sonar, and satellite position-finding systems – to help them steer a safe course. But in the past, none of these existed. Travellers out of sight of land or landmarks had to find other ways of **navigating** to help them reach their destinations and avoid dangerous obstacles on the way.

The most daring and successful early travellers, like the Phoenicians (from Lebanon) and Polynesian Islanders (who made long voyages across the Pacific Ocean), relied on the Sun during the daytime. It always rises in the east and sets in the west. By measuring its height above the horizon, they could calculate their **latitude** – that is, how far they had travelled north or south of the Equator.

▲ Early Phoenician travellers used the Sun by day and the stars by night to direct them on long voyages.

## Travelling in the dark

After the Sun set and it was dark, travellers had to use the stars to help them steer. This was not easy, because many stars and **constellations** appear to move across the night sky, as the Earth moves around the Sun. Every night, they seem to be in a slightly different place. But early sailors discovered that, with care, particular stars or constellations could be used to help them find directions. For example, travellers in the desert used the bright star Canopus to guide them.

◄ In the Northern hemisphere, travellers observed that the Pole Star stayed approximately above the North Pole all year long, and that two stars in the Plough constellation always pointed to it – even though the constellation itself appeared to move. You can see the Pole Star, labelled "Polvs".

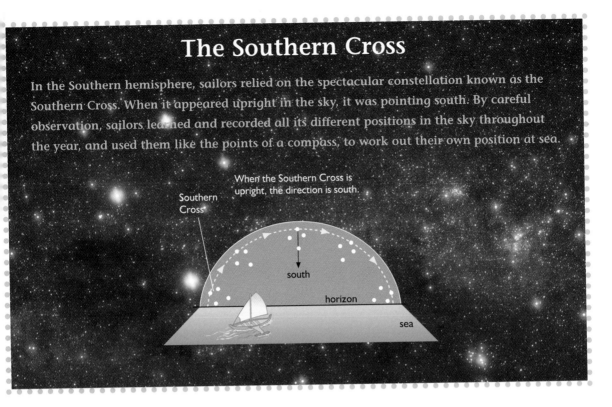

# The Southern Cross

In the Southern hemisphere, sailors relied on the spectacular constellation known as the Southern Cross. When it appeared upright in the sky, it was pointing south. By careful observation, sailors learned and recorded all its different positions in the sky throughout the year, and used them like the points of a compass, to work out their own position at sea.

When the Southern Cross is upright, the direction is south.

Southern Cross

south

horizon

sea

# Early observatories: Maragha and Samarkand

During the Middle Ages (about AD 1000–1500), some of the world's greatest star-gazers were Muslim scholars living in North Africa, Central Asia, and the Middle East. They were encouraged by Muslim rulers, who collected libraries of important scientific books from all over the known world, and paid for great **observatories**. These were purpose-built research centres for studying the Sun, Moon, and stars. The observatory at Maragha in Iran was built in 1259. It contained a huge range of astronomical instruments and was home to a library of over 40,000 books. At least 15 star-gazers worked at the Maragha observatory. One of the greatest Muslim

observatories established was at Samarkand, in Uzbekistan, Central Asia, in 1420. It housed a huge **sextant** (over 40 m high), which was used for measuring the changing positions of the Sun and the planets.

▲ The Ulugbek observatory at Samarkand, Uzbekistan

# Messages from the skies

Over the years, many people have believed that the stars were messengers, carrying good news or warnings of disaster. Sometimes, they believed these messages came from the gods in the sky; sometimes, they believed that the stars themselves had power to predict a person's future life.

▲ An Aztec holy fire ceremony

Some people believed that the regular appearance of stars in the sky was a sign that all was going well with the world. For example, the Aztecs of Mexico feared that, every 52 years, the world might come to an end. They asked their gods to send a message in the stars to reassure them that the world would continue. They put out all lights and fires while their priests scanned the skies. When the Evening Star appeared, they sacrificed a captive, and lit a holy fire on his chest. Then they sent messengers with flaming torches, lit from the fire, to bring new light and warmth to homes and temples.

In many civilizations, trained star-gazers, scholars, or priests acted as **interpreters** of star messages. In China, for example, there were scholars who became experts in heavenly patterns, which they called "tianwen". Their duty was to watch the skies for anything unusual among the stars and to work out what effect it might have on human lives.

▼ This armillary sphere was used by scholars at the observatory in Beijing, China, for determining the position of the stars.

One of the most famous plays in the world, Shakespeare's *Romeo and Juliet*, has two "star-crossed" lovers as its hero and heroine. Because the stars foretold an unhappy future, Romeo and Juliet were fated never to live together happily.

# The three wise men and the Star of Bethlehem

The Bible tells a story that links the birth of baby Jesus Christ with the appearance of a bright new star in the sky. It describes how three wise men travelled to Bethlehem, a Middle Eastern town. They were guided by a star, which led them onwards over deserts and mountains. In Bethlehem, they found the stable where Jesus was born, and offered him valuable gifts of gold, frankincense, and myrrh. Today, historians think that the wise men were probably star-gazers from Iran, who followed the Zoroastrian religion. The bright new star they saw above Bethlehem might have been a **comet**, a planet, or a **supernova** (see page 7).

 # Comets

Comets are balls of dust and ice that orbit the Sun. Each comet has a long tail and a globe-shaped head surrounded by a glowing halo. Comets appear in the sky at regular intervals, which can be anything from three years to a million years.

▶ This ancient Babylonian tablet describes the sighting of Halley's Comet in 164BC.

# Star forces

Many traditional stories about the stars claim that they can affect the health, character, success, and happiness of people born when they were visible in the sky. In medieval England, people thought that "dancing stars" seen by a mother giving birth would make a baby grow up to be light-hearted and energetic. The Bible records an ancient Middle Eastern belief that a group of seven stars called the Pleiades had a "sweet influence".

## Songs and sayings

Stars also feature today in many popular songs and sayings. For example, people often comment that someone who is restless was born "under a wandering star". They thank their "lucky stars" for unexpected good fortune, and make a wish when they see a shooting star, or catch sight of the first star in the evening sky. If someone suffers a blow on the head, they say he or she "saw stars". To "reach for the stars" means to aim high, or to be ambitious.

▶ The British Royal Air Force has a Latin motto "Per ardua ad astra", which means "Through hardship (or hard work) to the stars".

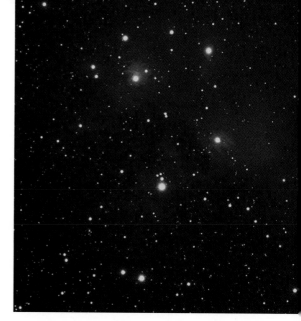

▲ The Pleiades are also called the Seven Sisters after an Ancient Greek myth that describes them as the daughters of the hero Atlas.

## Evil influences

For many peoples, stars were symbols of good fortune. But sometimes, they were thought to have an evil influence. The Ancient Romans believed that the Dog Days in July and August, when Sirius, the Dog Star, was visible, were always the hottest of the year. They were also times of sickness and madness, when poisonous snakes crept out of their hiding places to bite people and dogs. Altair, one of the brightest stars in the whole sky, was feared as a mischief-maker. The blue star, Algol, was also believed to be evil. Many different peoples called it the Demon Star.

Ancient religious teachers believed that the stars would show that the end of the world is approaching. For example, Jewish prophets described how the stars would fall from the sky at the end of the world.

# Science fiction

In science fiction, the world of the stars is used as a testing-ground, where heroes and villains can reveal their true nature, for good or evil. Popular films and TV dramas describe epic voyages by starship, and dramatic wars in space. They feature monstrous, inhuman **cyborgs**, robots, and aliens, but their heroes usually have admirable human qualities, such as courage and daring.

Since the late 20th century, space and the stars have also become favourite settings for computer and console games, and for games played on the Internet. Computer programmers and website designers use spectacular visual images gathered on real-life space exploration missions to add feelings of wonder and excitement to their games. Players need all their wits and skill to fight monsters and alien invaders from outer space and distant stars.

▼ Science-fiction writers often express our fear of the unknown by portraying other life forms as ugly and evil.

# Star words, star music

Stars have inspired many stories, poems, and songs. Some simply paint pictures of the stars in words, or describe the author's feelings as he or she gazes up at the night sky. But others are more complicated, with many layers of meaning. Many romantic writers make use of the stars to praise a lover or to describe loving feelings. Stars are sometimes used by other writers as symbols of courage and hope.

## Stars

Most merciful God
Look kindly upon
An impudent child
Who wants sitting on.
This evening late
I went to the door
And then to the gate
There were more stars – more
Than I could have expected,
Even I!
I was amazed,
Almighty, august!
I was utterly dazed,
Omnipotent! Just
In a word I was floored,
Good God of Hosts – Lord!
That at this time of day
They should still blaze away,
That thou hadst not rejected
Or at least circumspected
Their white silver beauty –
Was it spite? Was it duty?

*Katherine Mansfield*

[impudent = rude and naughty]
[august = praiseworthy]
[omnipotent = all-powerful]
[circumspected = had doubts about]

## A Summer Star

Now the thistles are flowering
And cicadas sit singing in the trees
Making shrill music by waggling their wings.
It is the season of exhausting hotness
When goats look plump and well fed
And wine tastes sweetest.
Women are more loving
But men feel weak
Because the Dog-Star Sirius scorches them from head to foot
And their bodies are all dried up by its heat.

▲ This is part of a long poem by Hesiod, called "Works and Days". Hesiod lived in Ancient Greece around 700 BC.

# The Night has a Thousand Eyes

The night has a thousand eyes,
    And the day but one;
Yet the light of a bright world dies
    When day is done.

The mind has a thousand eyes,
    And the heart but one;
Yet the light of a whole life dies
    When love is done.

*Francis William Bourdillion*

▲ Romantic writers often describe their heroine's eyes as "shining like stars", or say that someone who has fallen in love "has stars in their eyes".

◀ One night, the British poet, Lord Byron, caught sight of a beautiful dark-haired, dark-eyed girl wearing a black dress covered in sequins – hundreds of tiny mirrors that sparkled like stars as she moved. He was so impressed by the sight that he wrote a poem to praise her. Here is how it begins:

## She Walks in Beauty

She walks in beauty like the night
Of cloudless climes and starry skies,
And all that's best of dark and bright
Meet in her aspect and her eyes;
Thus mellowed in the tender light
Which heaven to gaudy day denies.

*Lord Byron*

[climes = weather]
[aspect = appearance]
[gaudy = bright]

# Gods and humans

Priests and people from many different civilizations have looked to the stars for signs of their gods. For example, 600 years ago, the Incas of South America studied the dark spaces of the Mayu (Heavenly River, or Milky Way). They hoped to see their rain god there, outlined by starlight. They also named their queen "Coya", which means "star", and honoured her as a goddess. In Ancient Persia (now Iran), stars were believed to be the eyes of Mithras, the god of light. In India, traditional stories tell how shooting stars announced the birth of the **Hindu** fire-god, Agni, and of the **Buddha**.

▲ In the Bible, angels are sometimes described as stars, and the starry night sky as a host of heavenly spirits.

▲ Seen on starry nights in the far north, the Northern Lights have inspired many legends on the theme of life after death.

## Stars and spirits

Stars and angels (messengers from God) are linked in traditional stories from Muslim Arabia. They describe shooting stars as fireballs thrown by angels to drive away inquisitive djinns (evil desert spirits) who climbed up the **constellations** to try to catch a glimpse of Paradise.

The words "gone to join the stars" can be a gentle way of saying that someone has died. In many cultures, stars are thought to be the spirits of dead ancestors. For example, the Chukchi of Siberia, and other Arctic peoples, traditionally believed that dead peoples' spirits went to live in camps in the kingdom of the Pole Star.

Stars have also been seen as the souls of unborn children, waiting to have a life on Earth, or as guardian spirits, taking care of living men and women. Many native peoples of North America believed that each living creature was linked at birth to their own particular star, which watched over them all the time.

# Star patterns everywhere

Star shapes and star patterns are all around us. We can see them in an amazing variety of places. In nature, we find microscopic starry **plankton** and bacteria, starfish, snowflakes, and many star-shaped blooms, such as star-gazer lilies and beautiful blue borage, which is also called star-flower.

Because of their sparkle and shine, spectacular crystals and precious stones are often called stars. The Star of Africa is a massive diamond, discovered in 1869. The Star of India is another huge diamond, now displayed in the Queen of England's crown as a sign of her royal power.

Stars are often used as signs of rank – a top army officer in the USA is known as a five-star general because of the stars sewn on his uniform sleeve. Also in the USA, sheriffs and other law-keepers wear a star-shaped badge.

Stars are also popular with artists and craftworkers in many different countries. They can have four, five, six, seven, or eight points, depending on local traditions and beliefs.

▲ A star-patterned quilt made in the USA in the mid-19th century

▼ The Queen's crown, with the Star of India set in the front

◀ An American sheriff's badge

▶ The five stars worn by American army generals

# Flags and stamps

For many centuries, stars have been one of the most popular symbols used on national banners and flags. They are said to be signs of watchfulness, striving, and strength. Around 300 BC, the Macedonian ruler Alexander the Great, who conquered an empire in India and the Middle East, used the star as the symbol of his kingdom. Today, stars appear on the flags, coins, and postage stamps of many Islamic nations, including Turkey and Pakistan. The European Union flag also has a circle of golden-yellow stars on a blue background representing the sky.

## The Star of David

The star is an ancient Jewish symbol. A five-pointed star was used as the seal of the famous Jewish king, Solomon, who ruled from around 970–930 BC. Another great Jewish king, David (who ruled around 1010–970 BC), used a six-pointed star. Later, this became a badge of identification for all Jewish people.

◀ Today, a blue Star of David forms part of the Israeli national flag.

European Union

Burundi

USA

Turkey

Pakistan

North Korea

Iraq

Cameroon

New Zealand

Malaysia

Chile

Singapore

## The Stars and Stripes

The Stars and Stripes is the popular name for the flag of the United States of America. (It is also known as the Star-Spangled Banner or Old Glory.) The stripes stand for the original 13 states that broke away from British **colonial rule** in 1773. The stars represent all the states of the Union today – there are now 50.

# Glossary

**astrologer** Someone who studies the Sun, Moon, planets, and stars in the belief that they influence human lives.

**astronomer** A scientist who studies space and all that it contains.

**astronomy** The scientific study of the Sun, Moon, planets, and stars.

**atmosphere** Layers of gases that surround a planet and protect it from radiation.

**Buddha** "The Enlightened One" – a name given to a religious teacher who lived in India around 500BC. His followers are known as Buddhists.

**centaur** A creature from Ancient Greek mythology – half man, half horse.

**colonial rule** Rule of a weaker country by a stronger one. The ruling country imposes its own laws and social customs, and exploits the weaker country's resources.

**comet** A massive ball of dust and ice that orbits the Sun. Most comets have long tails.

**constellation** A group of stars linked together by observers on the Earth, who imagine that they form pictures in the sky.

**cupbearer** A servant who carried cups full of drink to diners at a feast.

**cyborg** A science-fiction monster, part human, part machine.

**galaxy** A collection of stars, dust, and gas held together by gravity. Galaxies have many different shapes, and may group together to form clusters.

**gravity** The natural force that attracts objects towards each other.

**Hindu** To do with the Hindu religion, an ancient religion from India.

**host** An army.

**interpreters** Experts who translate from one language into another, or who explain difficult or secret knowledge to other people.

**latitude** The distance north or south of an imaginary line around the centre of the Earth, called the Equator.

**Milky Way** A spiral-shaped galaxy that contains our Solar System – that is, the Sun and all the planets that orbit it – together with many millions of stars.

**navigating** Plotting and steering a course at sea.

**neutron star** A very small, very hot, and extremely dense star, formed when a supernova explosion ends.

**nuclear reaction** A process in which the nucleus (core) of an atom splits, releasing vast amounts of energy.

**observatory** A building where astronomers use telescopes and other scientific instruments to study space.

**orbit** The path of a moon or spacecraft around a planet, or a planet around the Sun.

**plankton** Microscopic plants and animals that live in sea-water.

**radiation** Heat and light energy.

**sextant** A scientific instrument used to measure the position of the Sun, Moon, or stars above the horizon.

**Shabbat** The Jewish holy day that lasts from Friday evening to Saturday evening.

**singularity** A region of space where the normal laws of science do not work.

**supernova** A huge, very hot explosion that happens when a massive star collapses.

**superstition** Unscientific belief in supernatural happenings.

**white dwarf** A very small, very dense star that is nearing the end of its life.

**zodiac** An imaginary path travelled by the Sun across the sky. It appears to pass through 12 constellations known as "signs of the zodiac". Some people think they influence events on Earth.

# Books for further reading

Heather Couper and Nigel Henbest, *Space Encyclopedia* (Dorling Kindersley, 1999)

Eva M Hans, *Spinning Through Space – Comets and Asteroids* (Hodder Wayland, 2000)

Eva M Hans, *Spinning Through Space – Constellations* (Hodder Wayland, 2000)

D Lambert, *New View – Stars and Planets* (Watts, 2001)

Patrick Moore, *Philip's Guide to the Stars and Planets* (Chancellor Press, 2001)

Rhoda Nottridge, *Skywatch* (Collins, 1991)

Nikki Siegen-Smith (ed), *A Pocketful of Stars – poems about the night* (Barefoot Books, 1999)

Usborne Spotters' Guides – *The Night Sky* (Usborne, 2000)

# Index